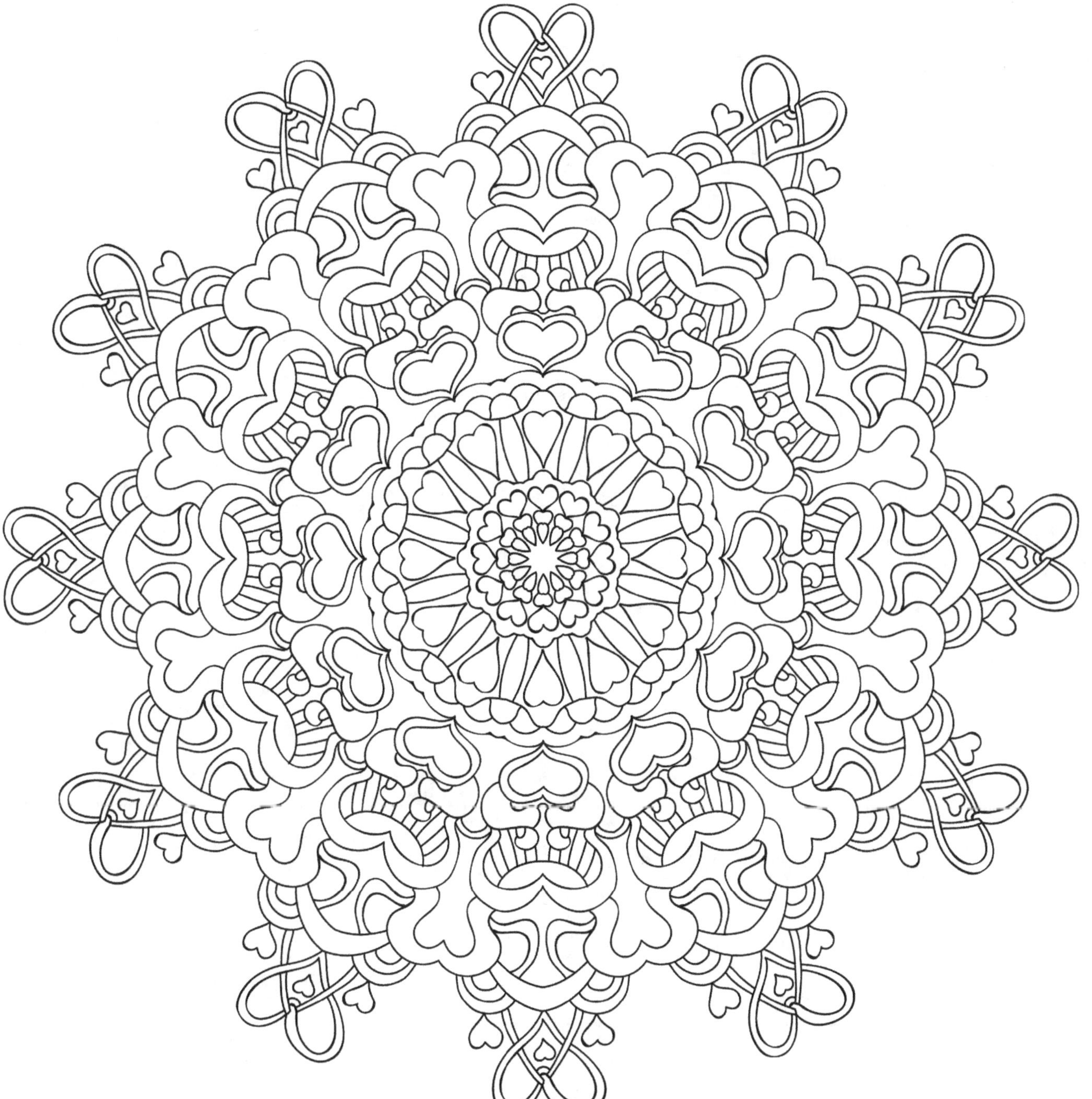

ISBN: 978-1523353231
by: Adult Coloring Book Sets
(Illustrated by: Joshua Lazana Lagman and Jade Villaremo)

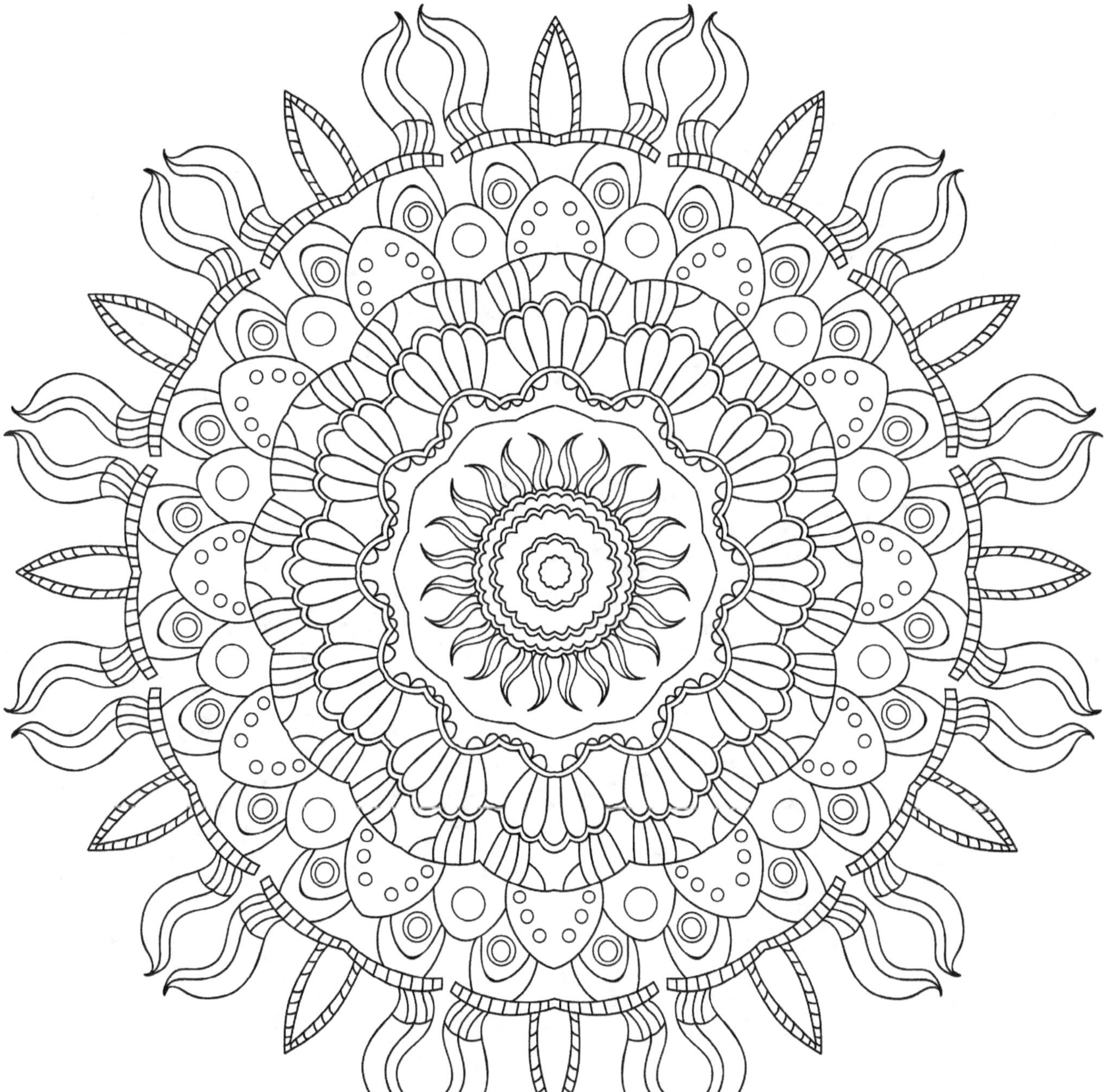

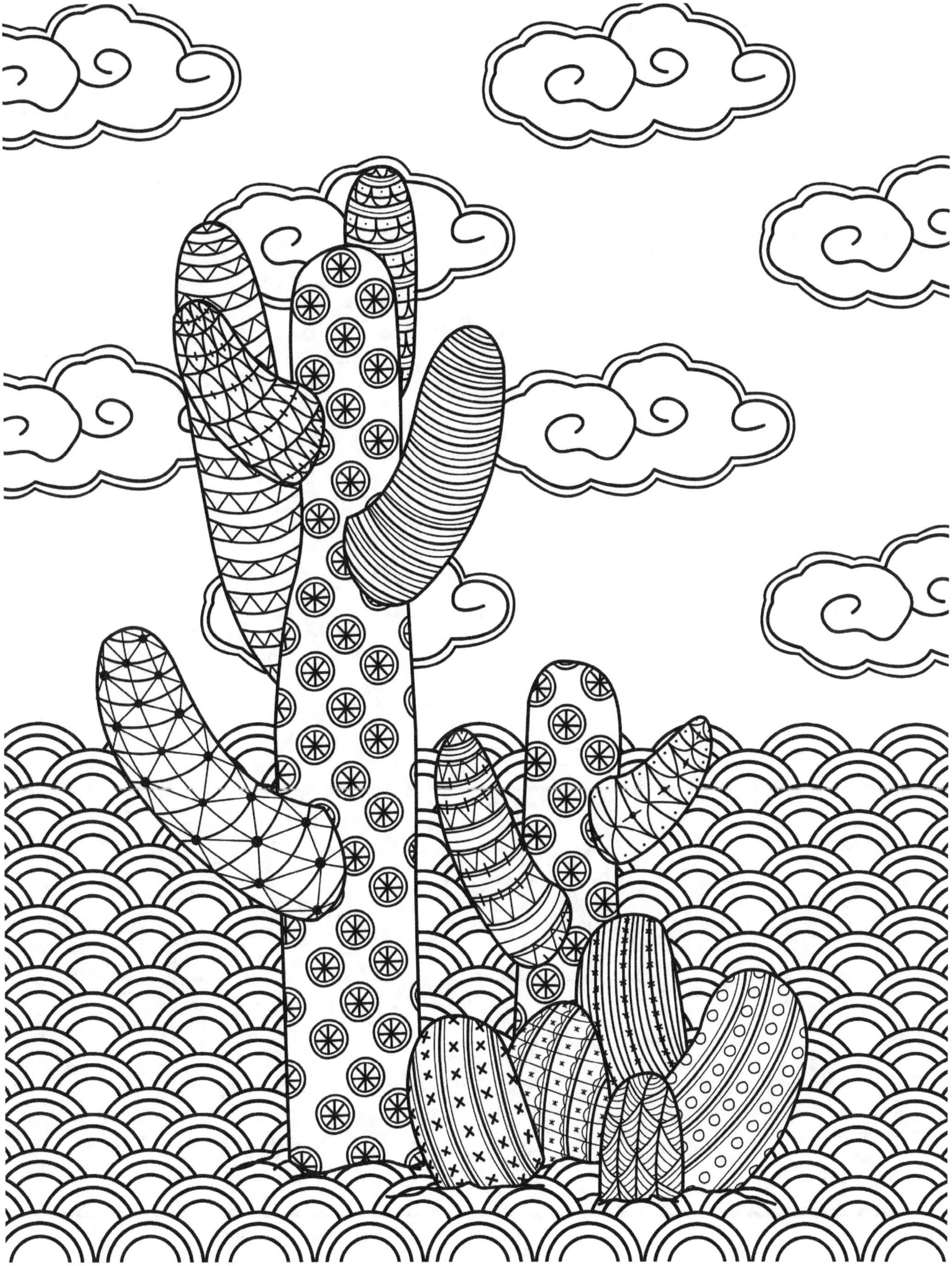

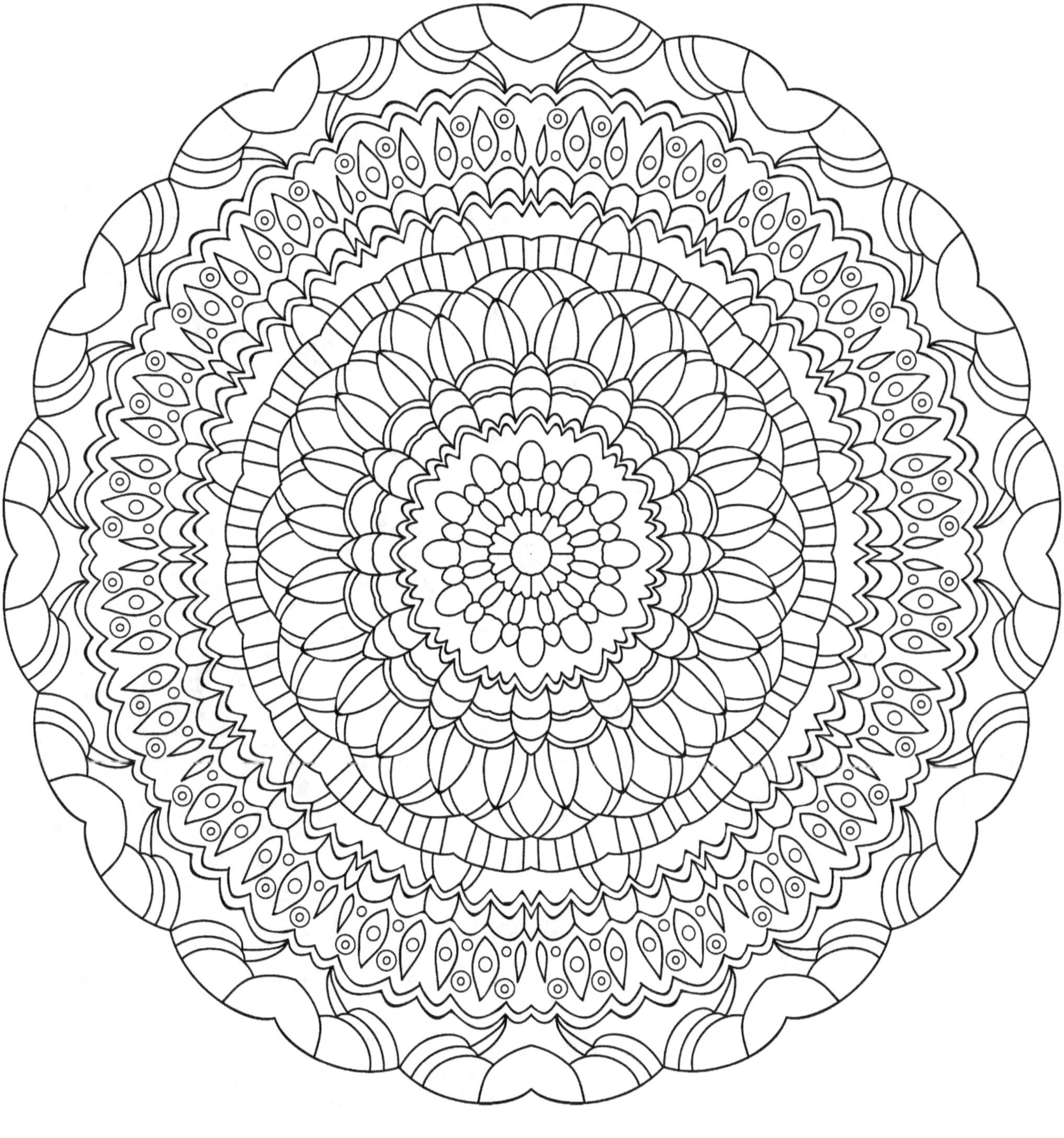

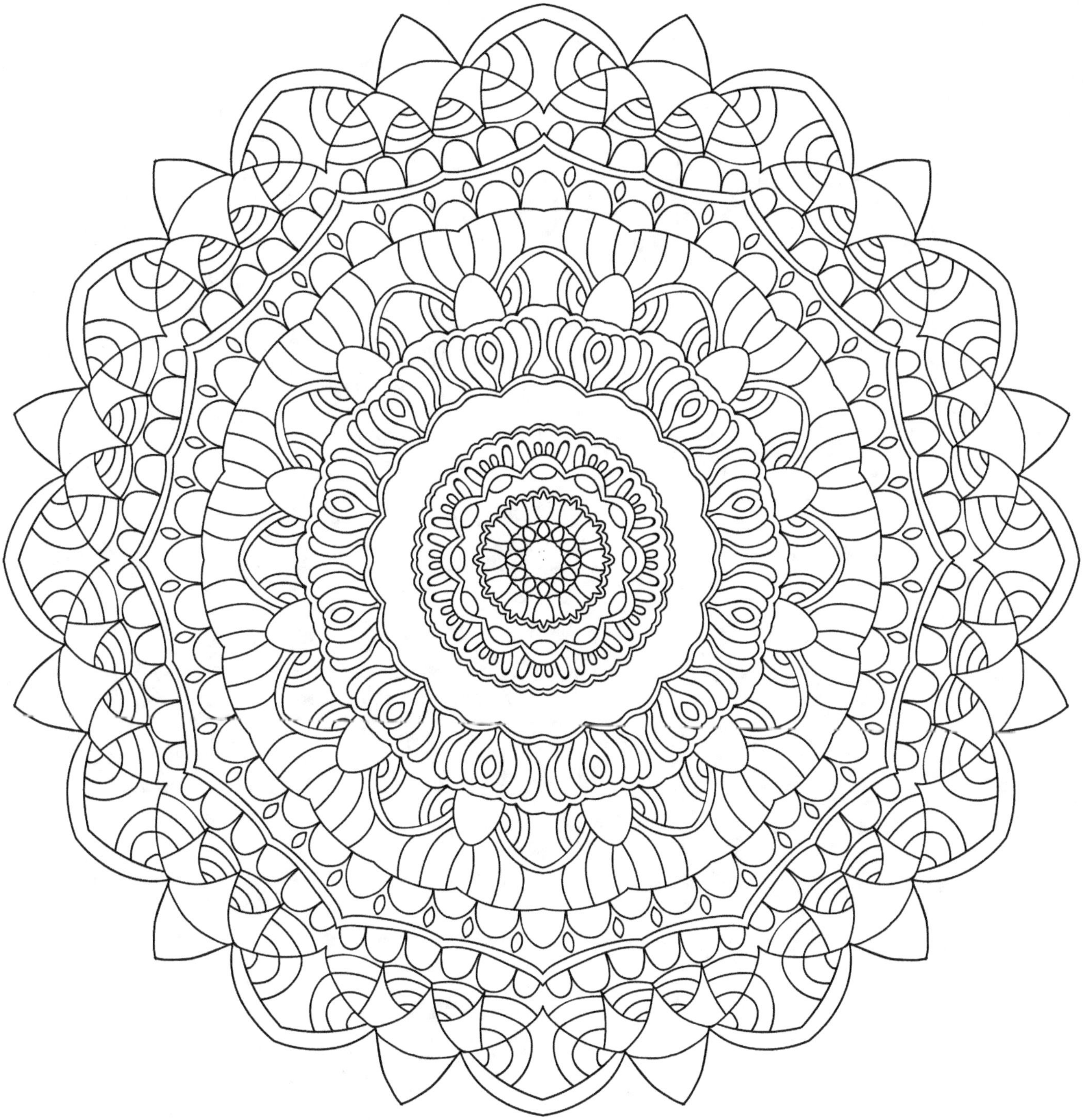

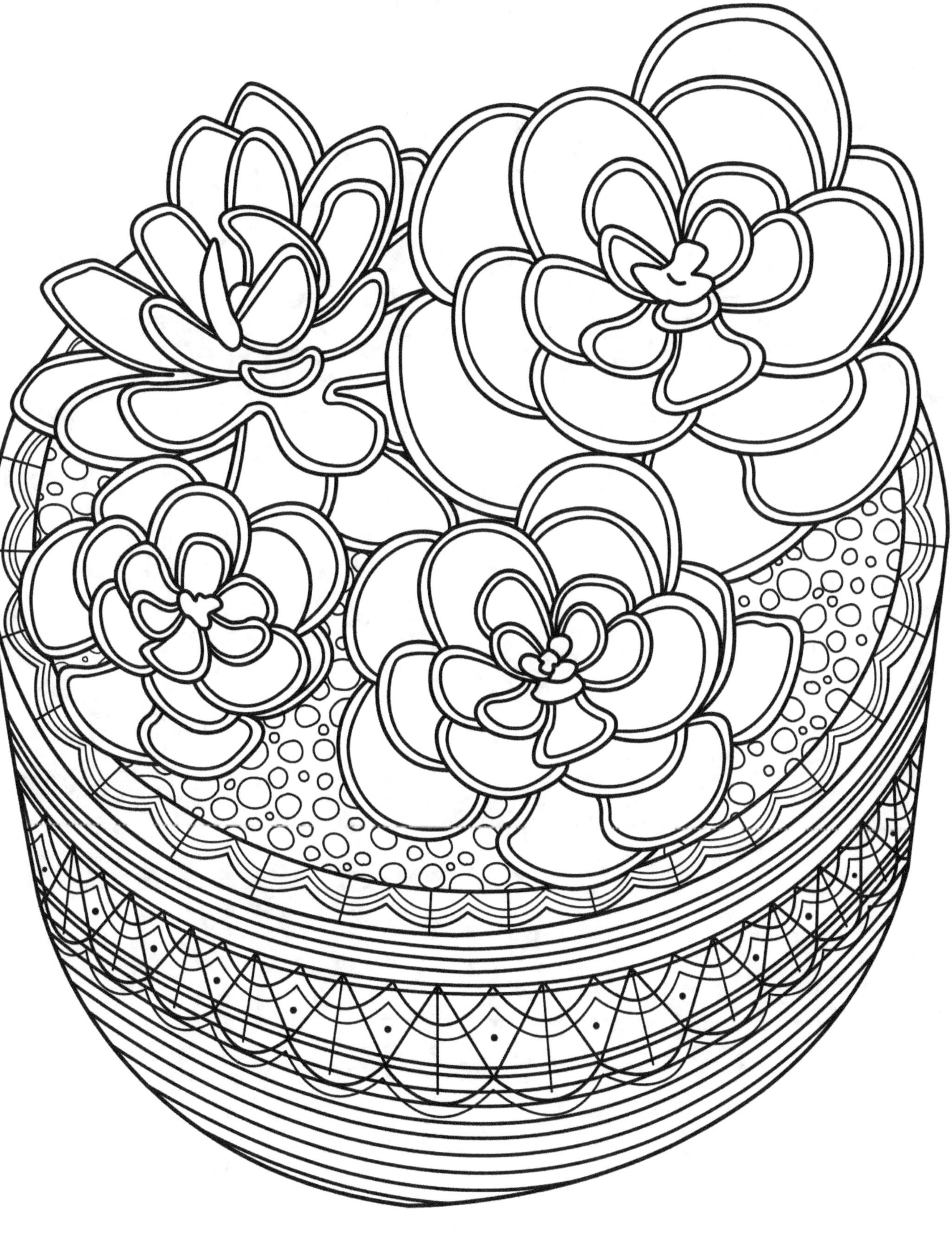

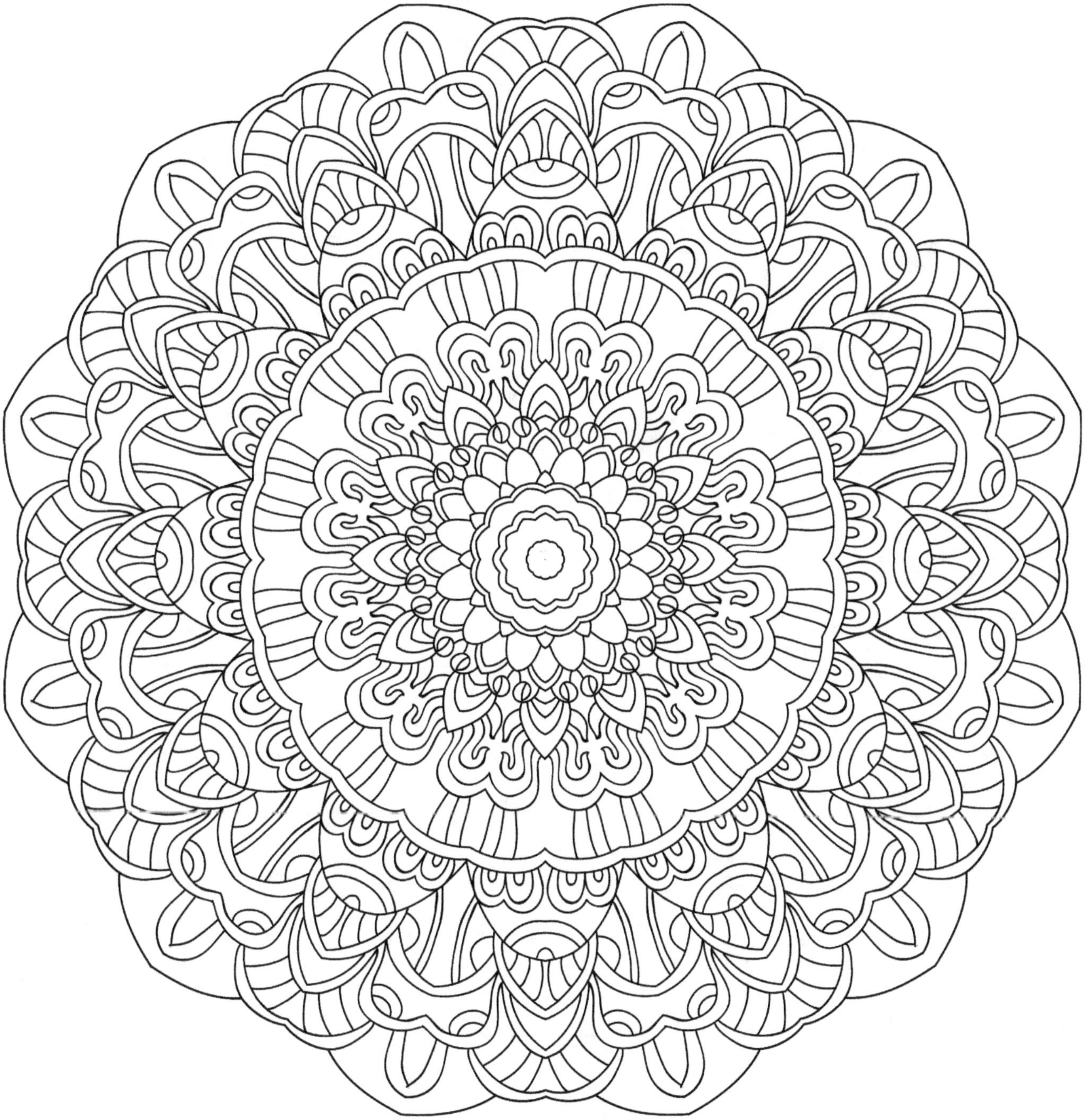

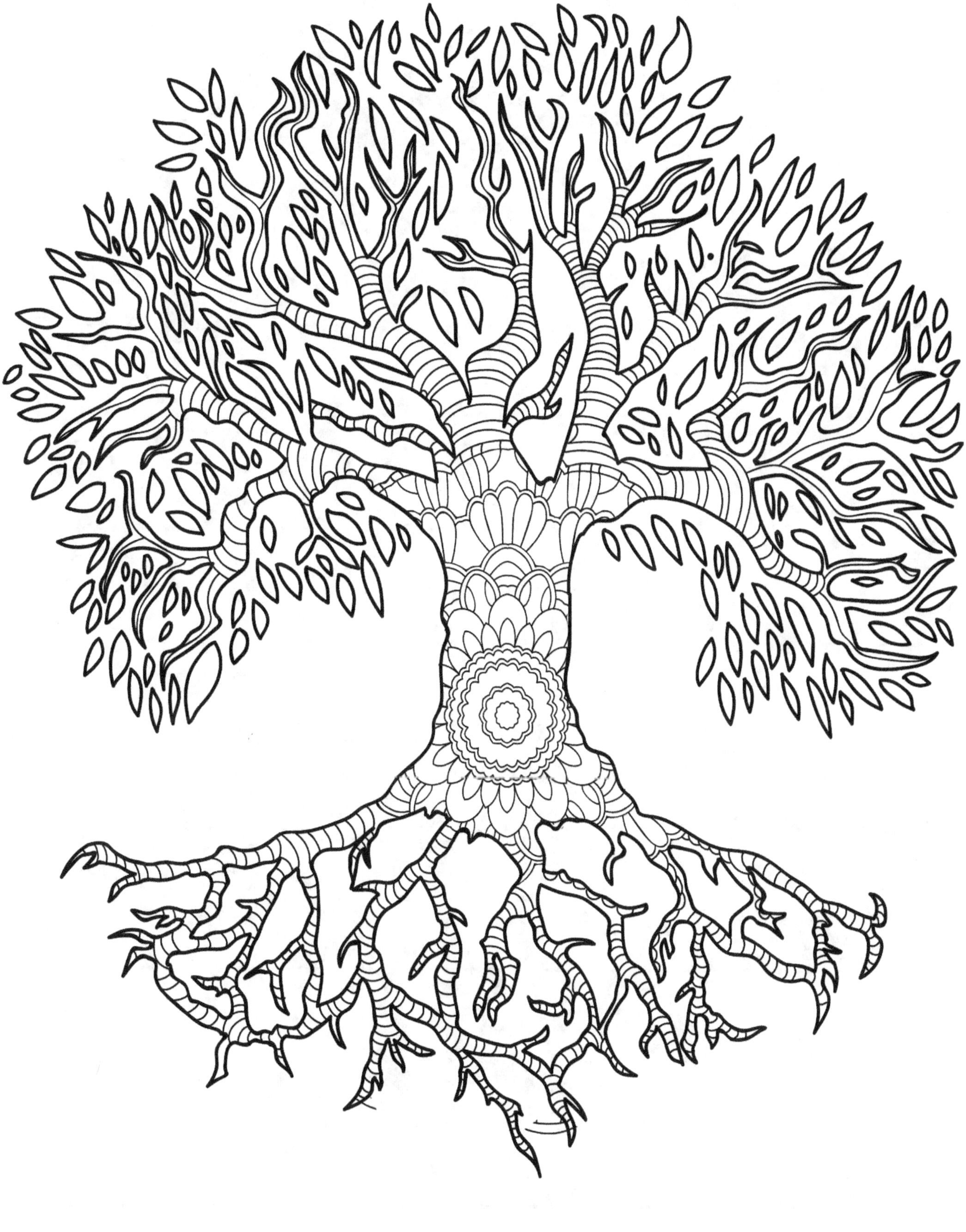

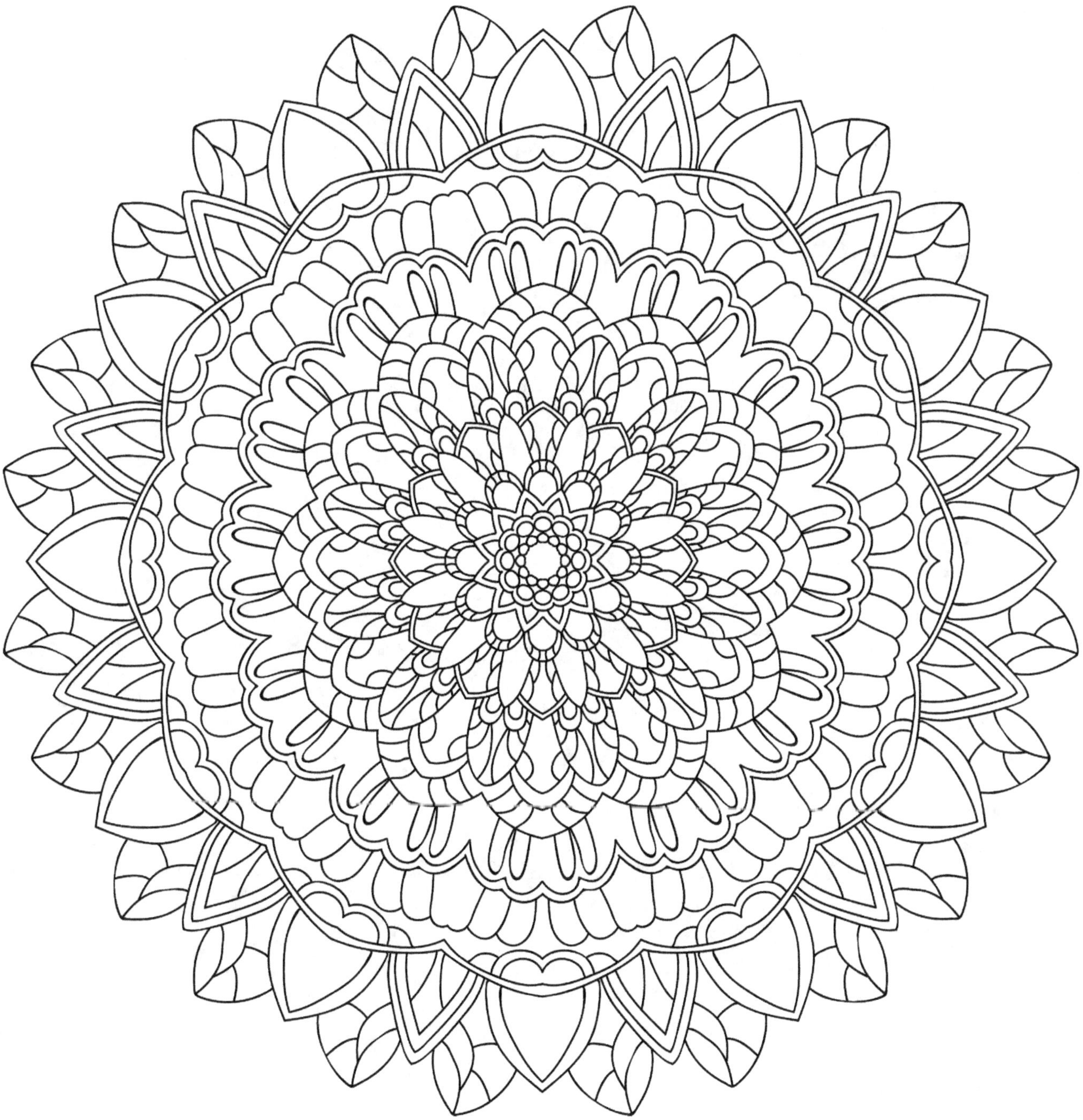

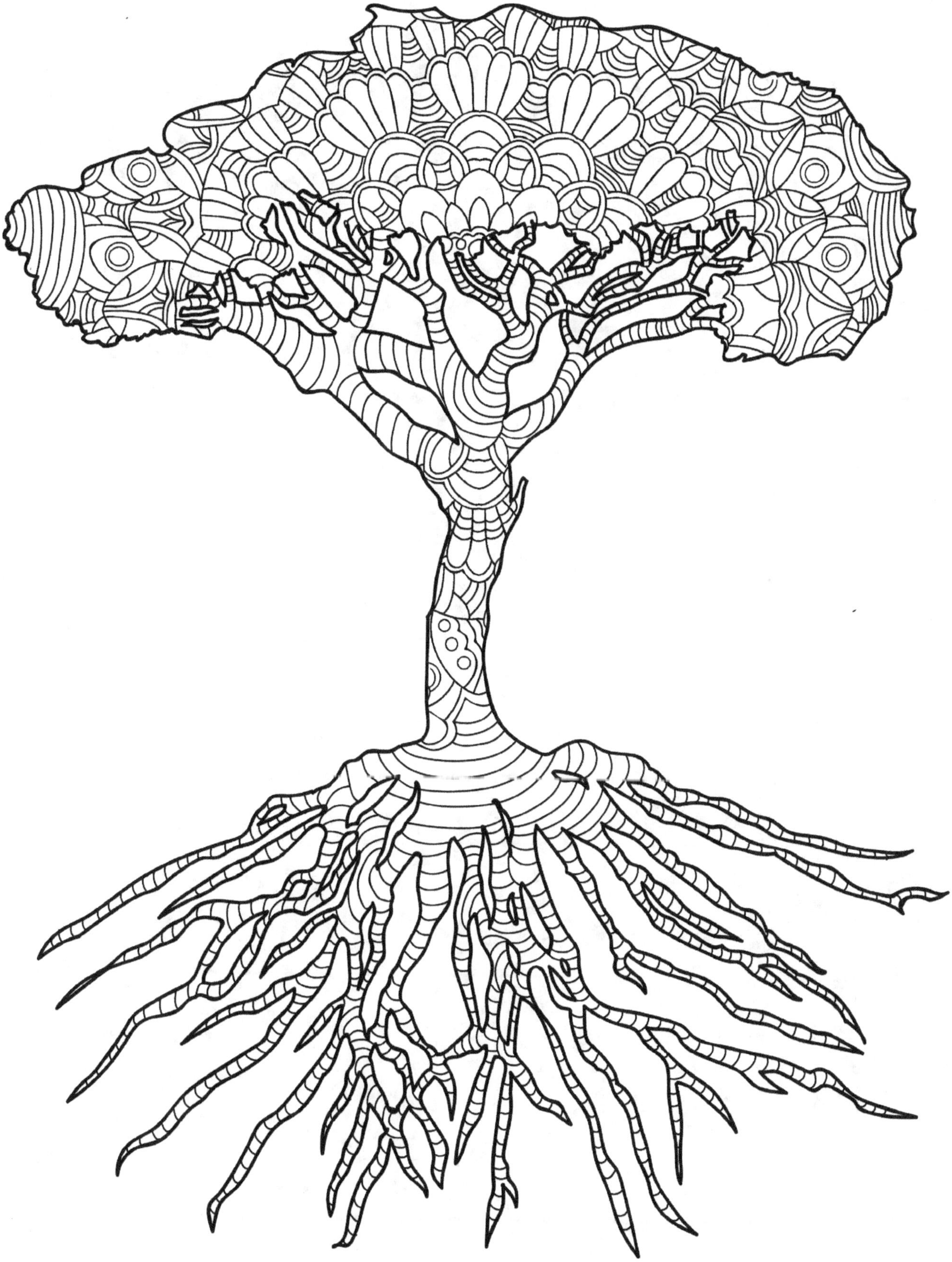

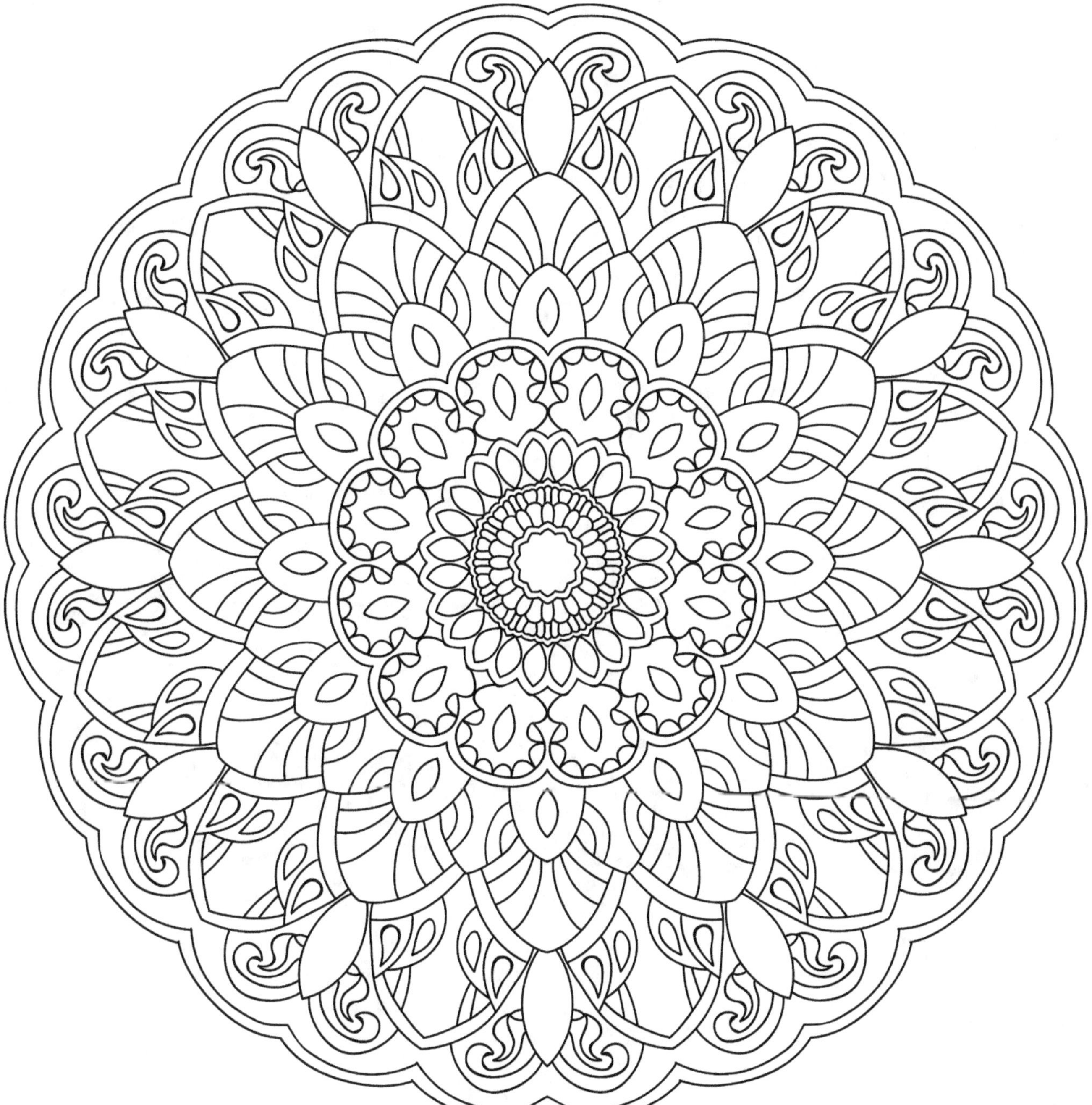

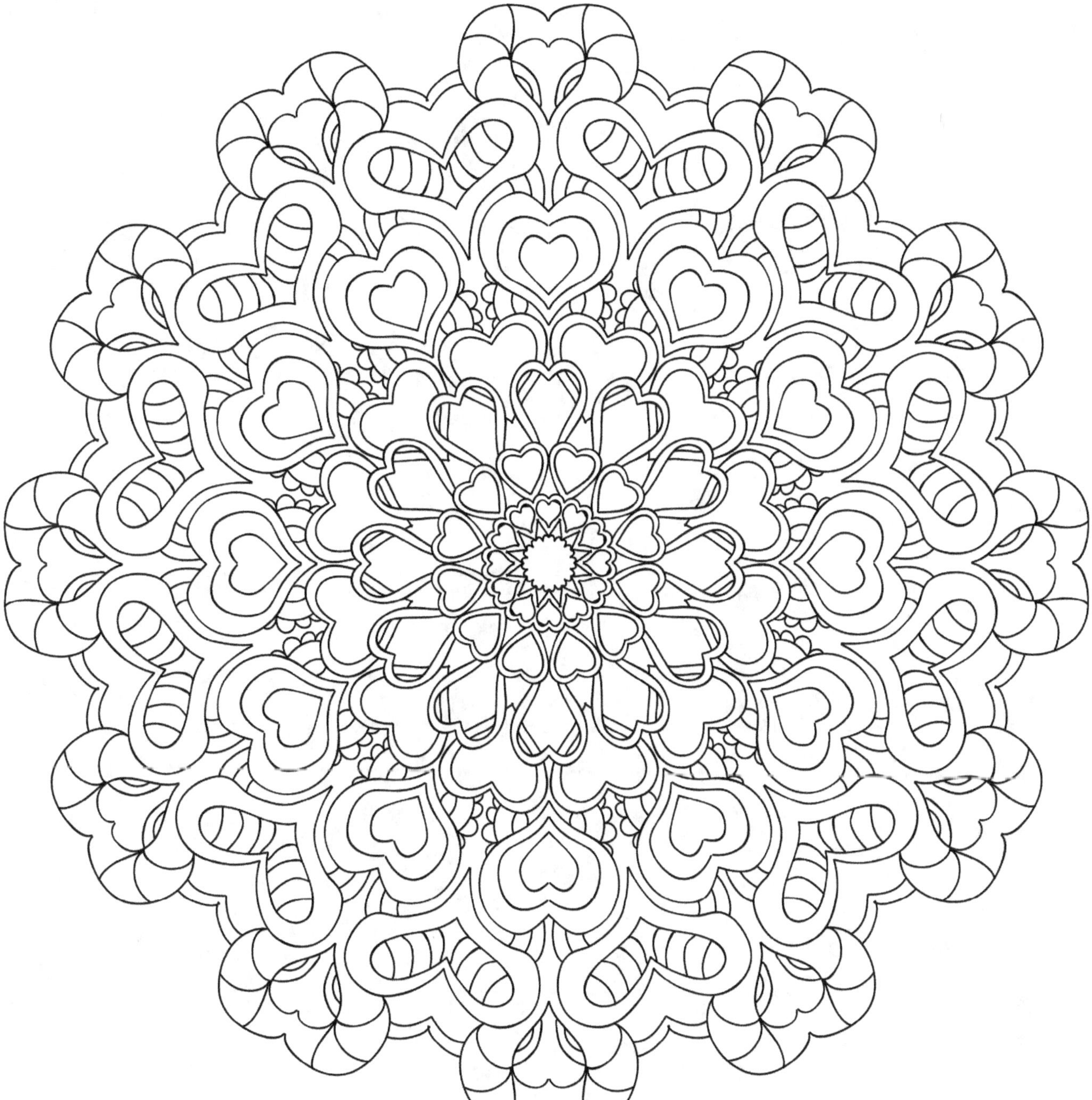

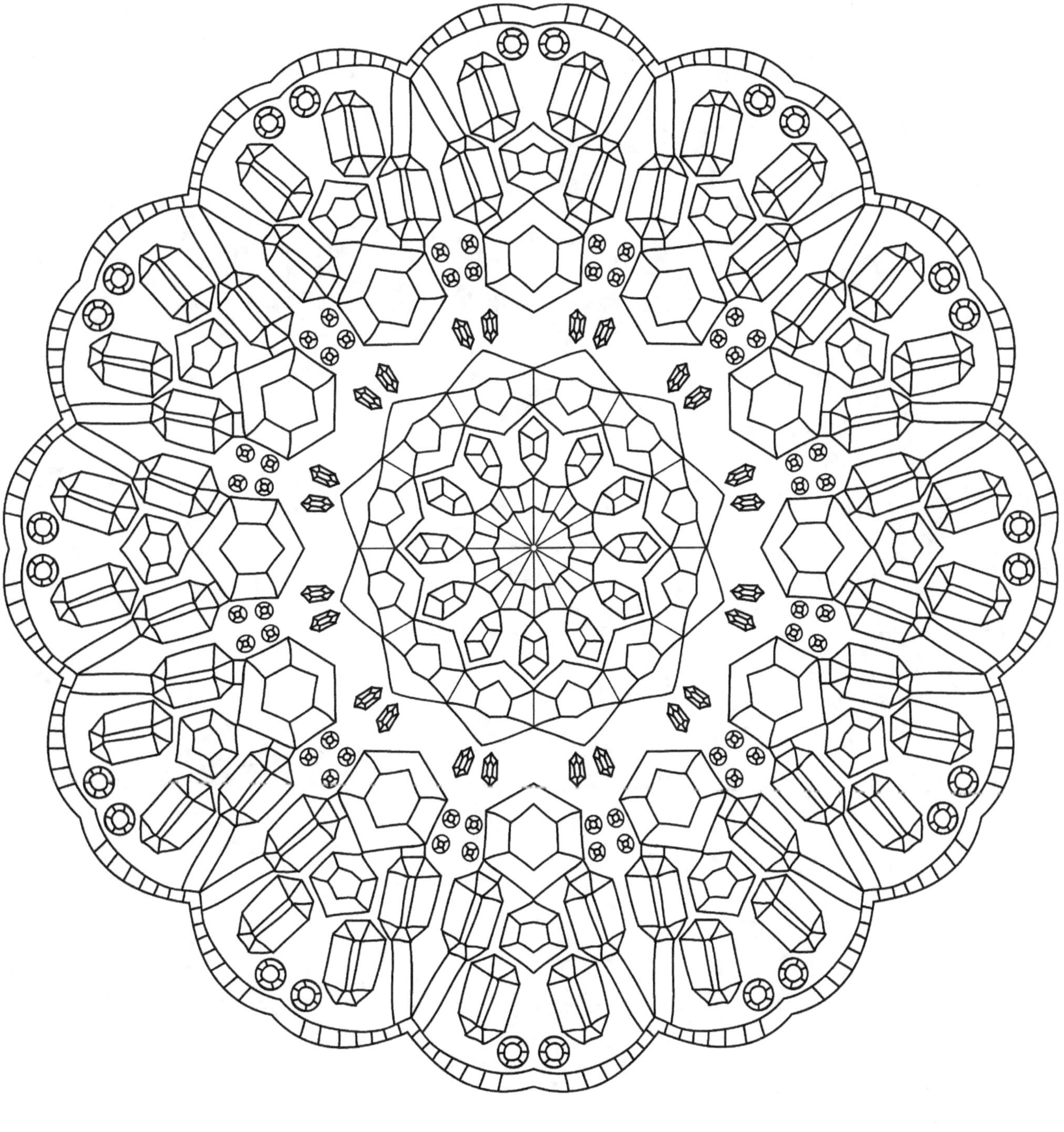

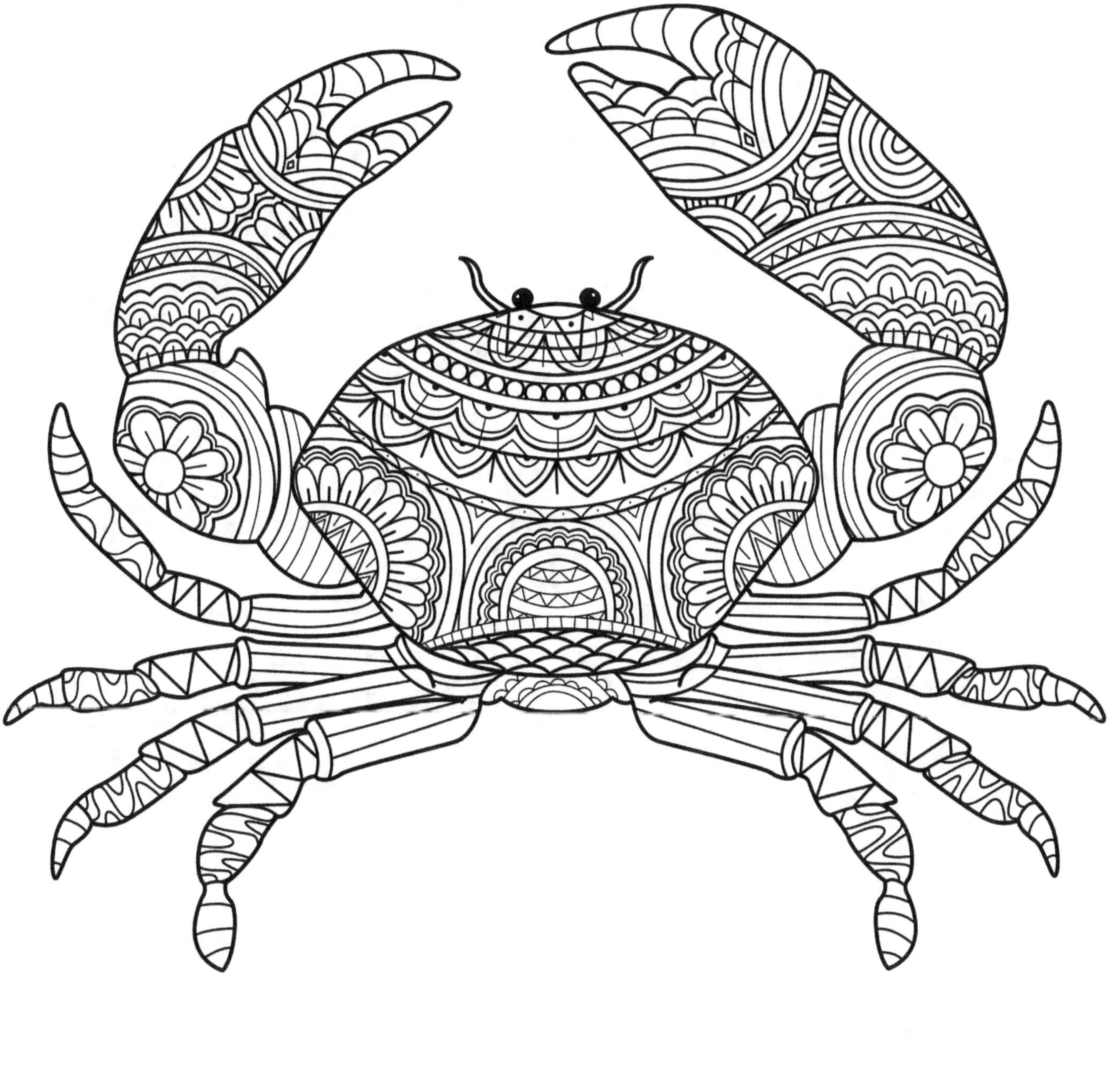

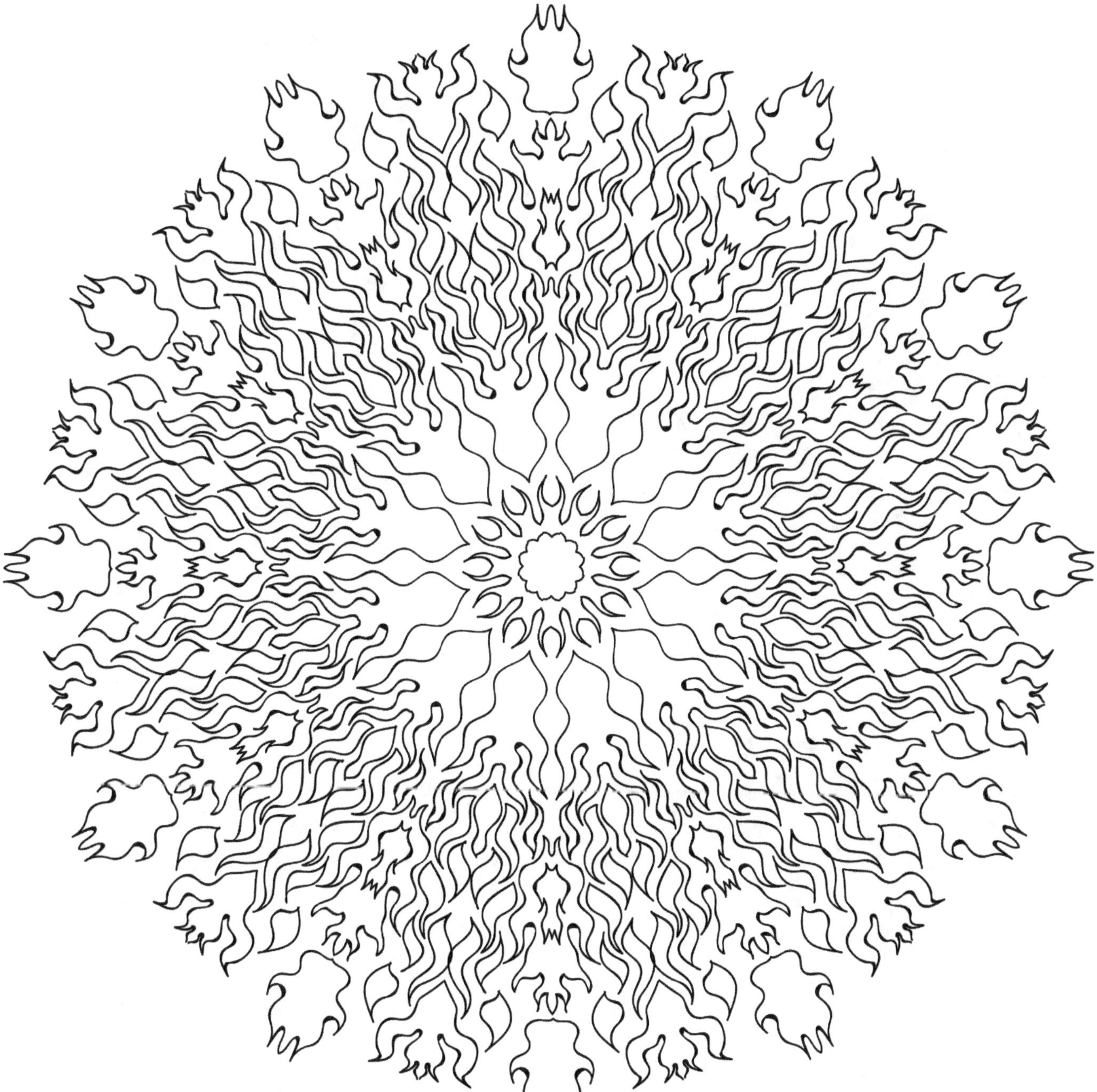

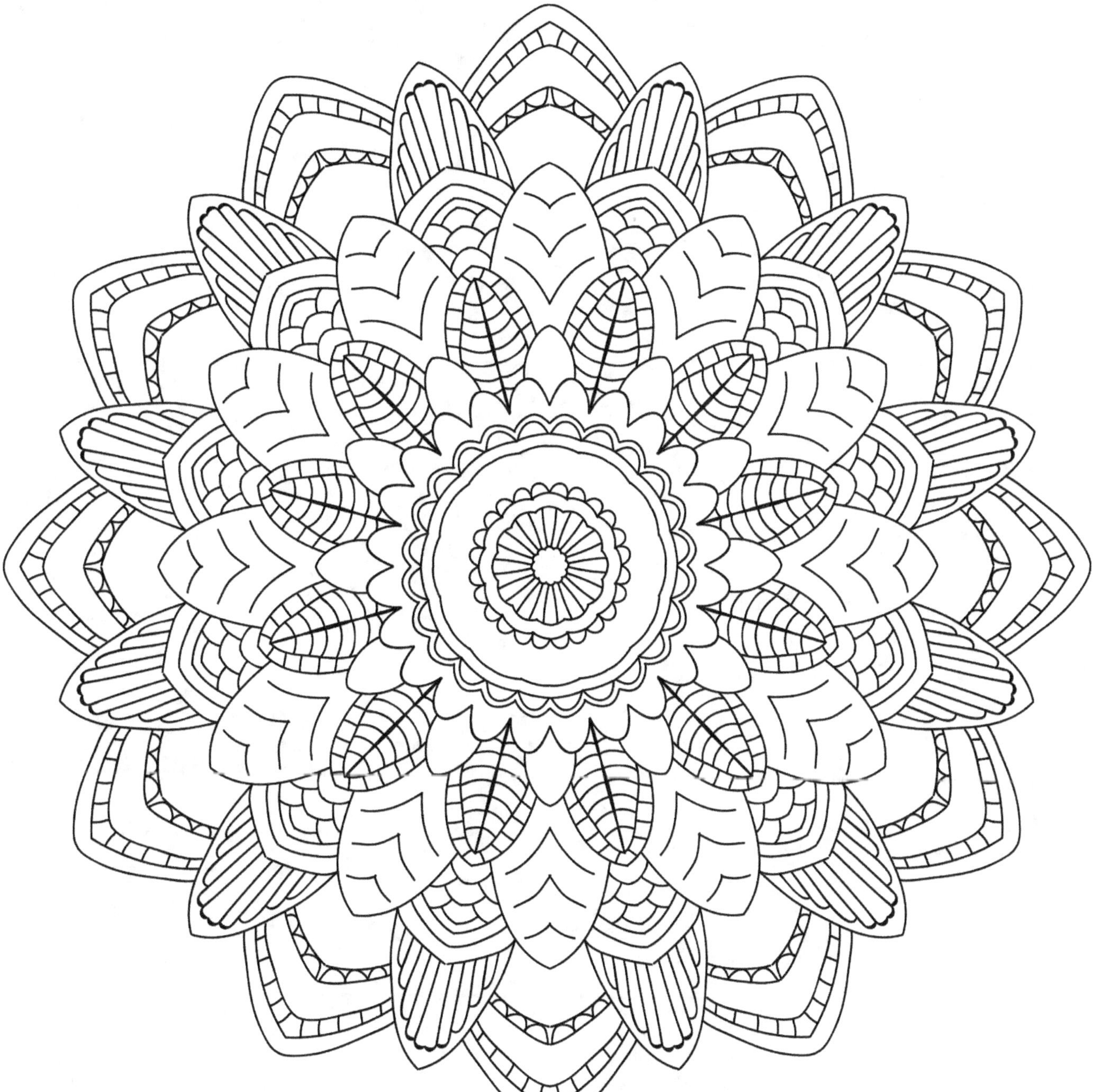

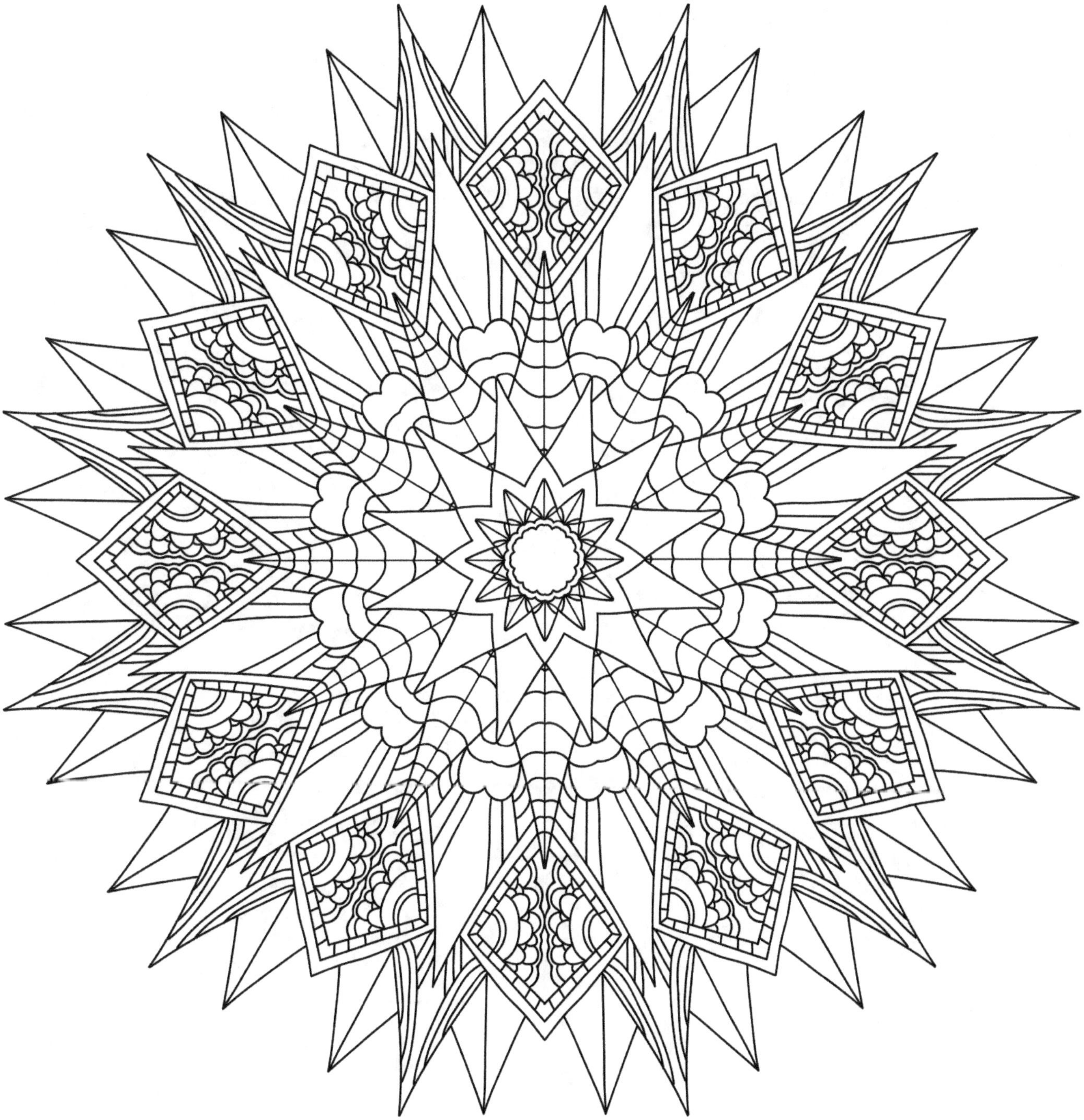

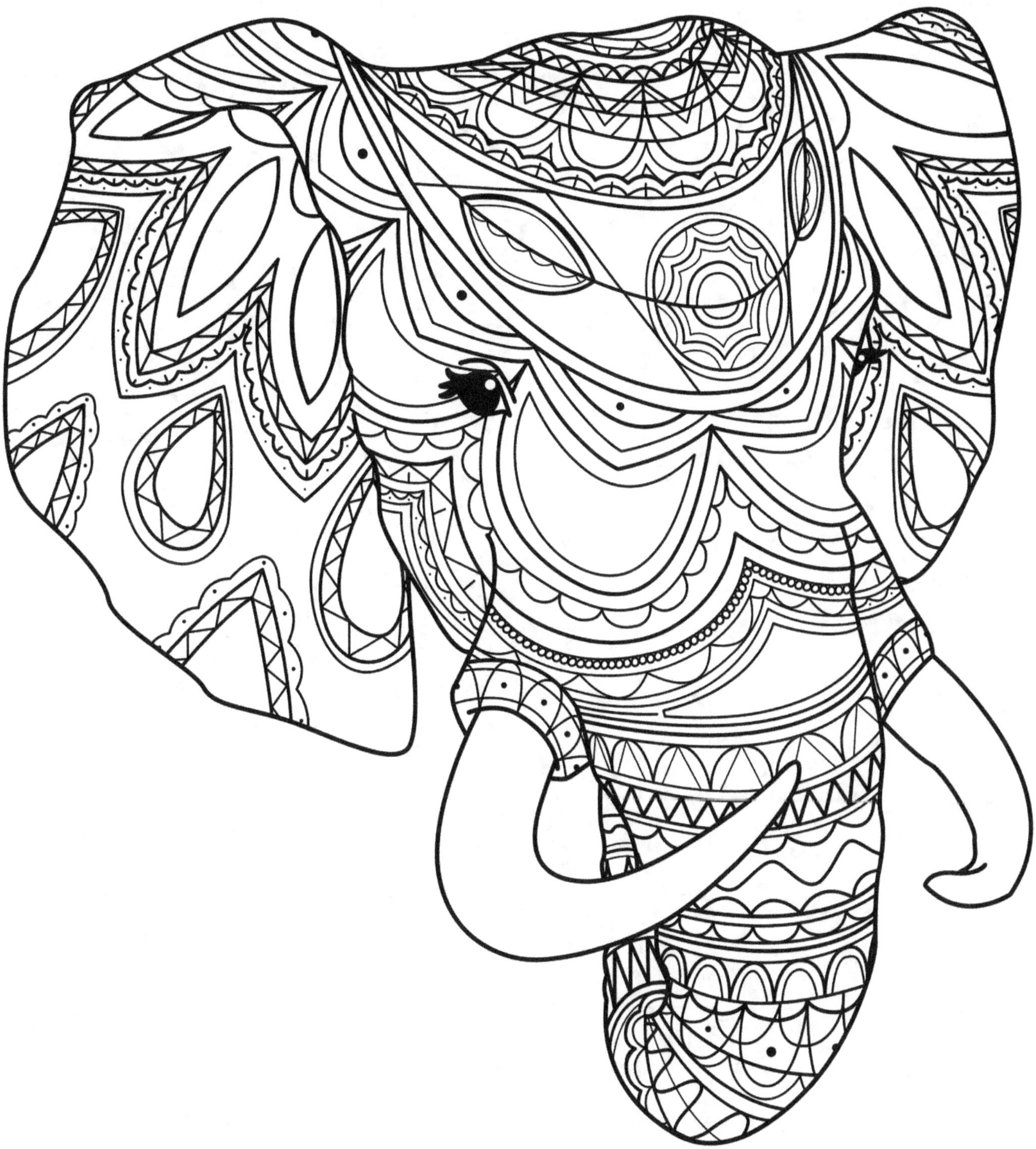

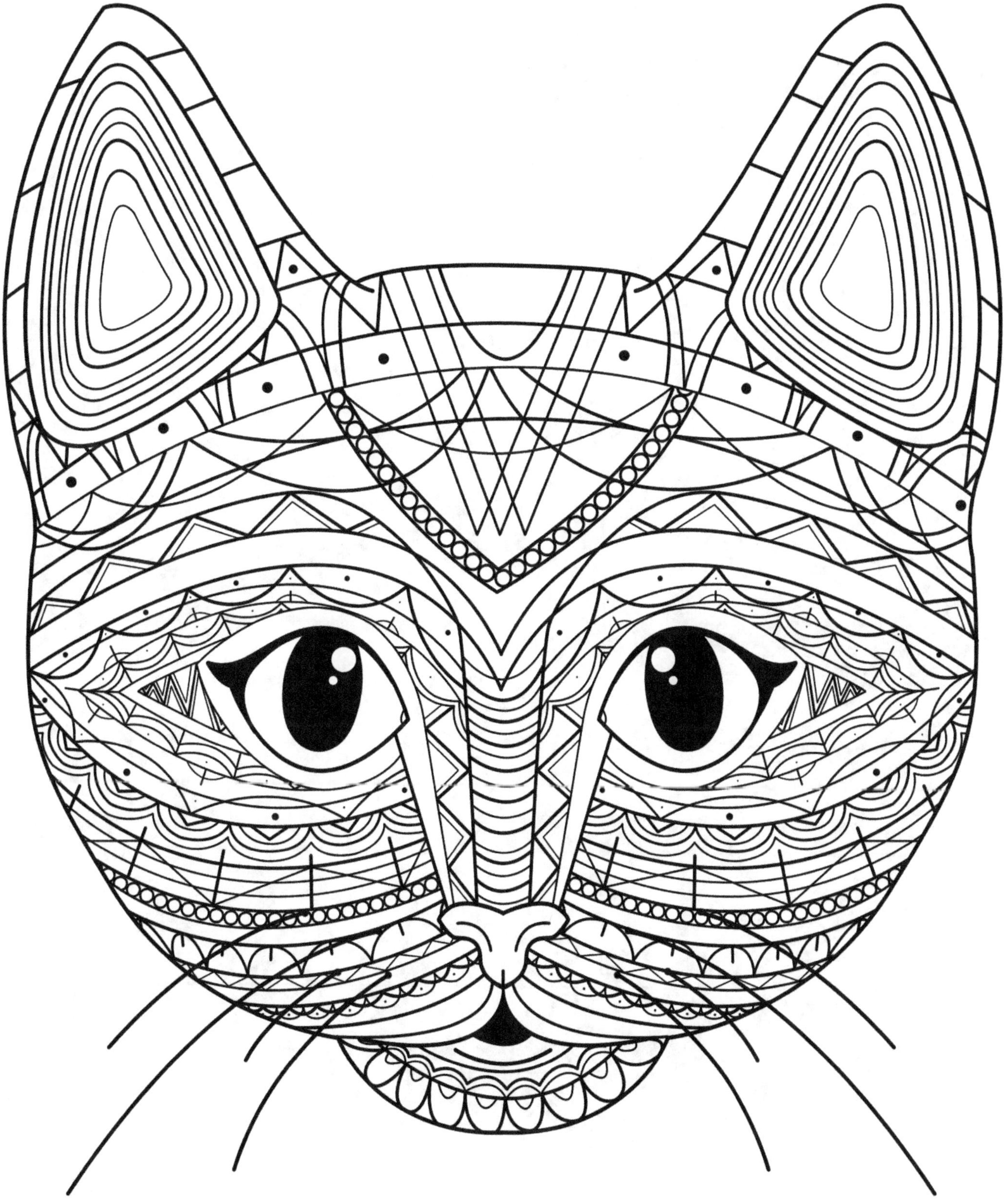

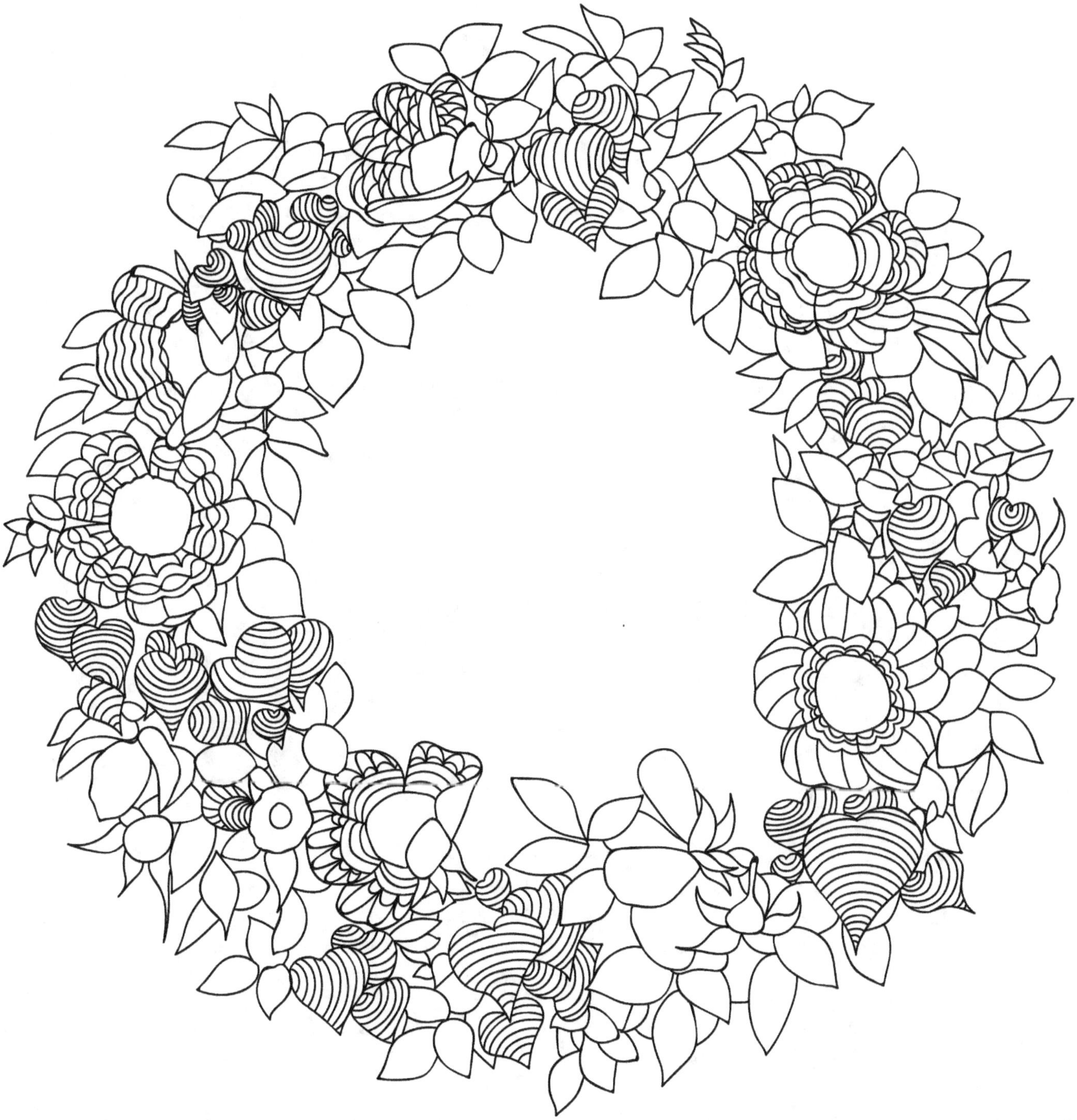

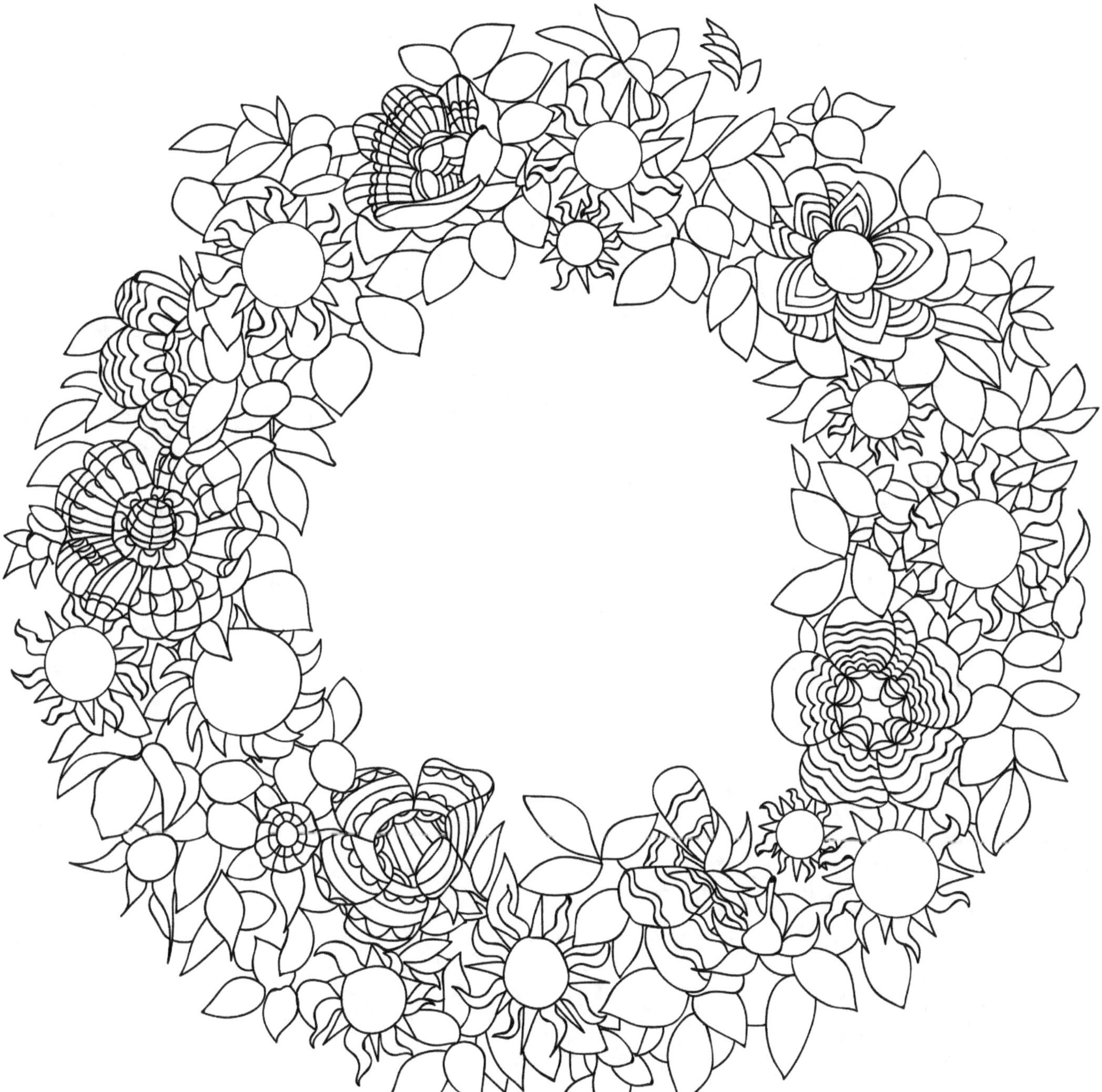

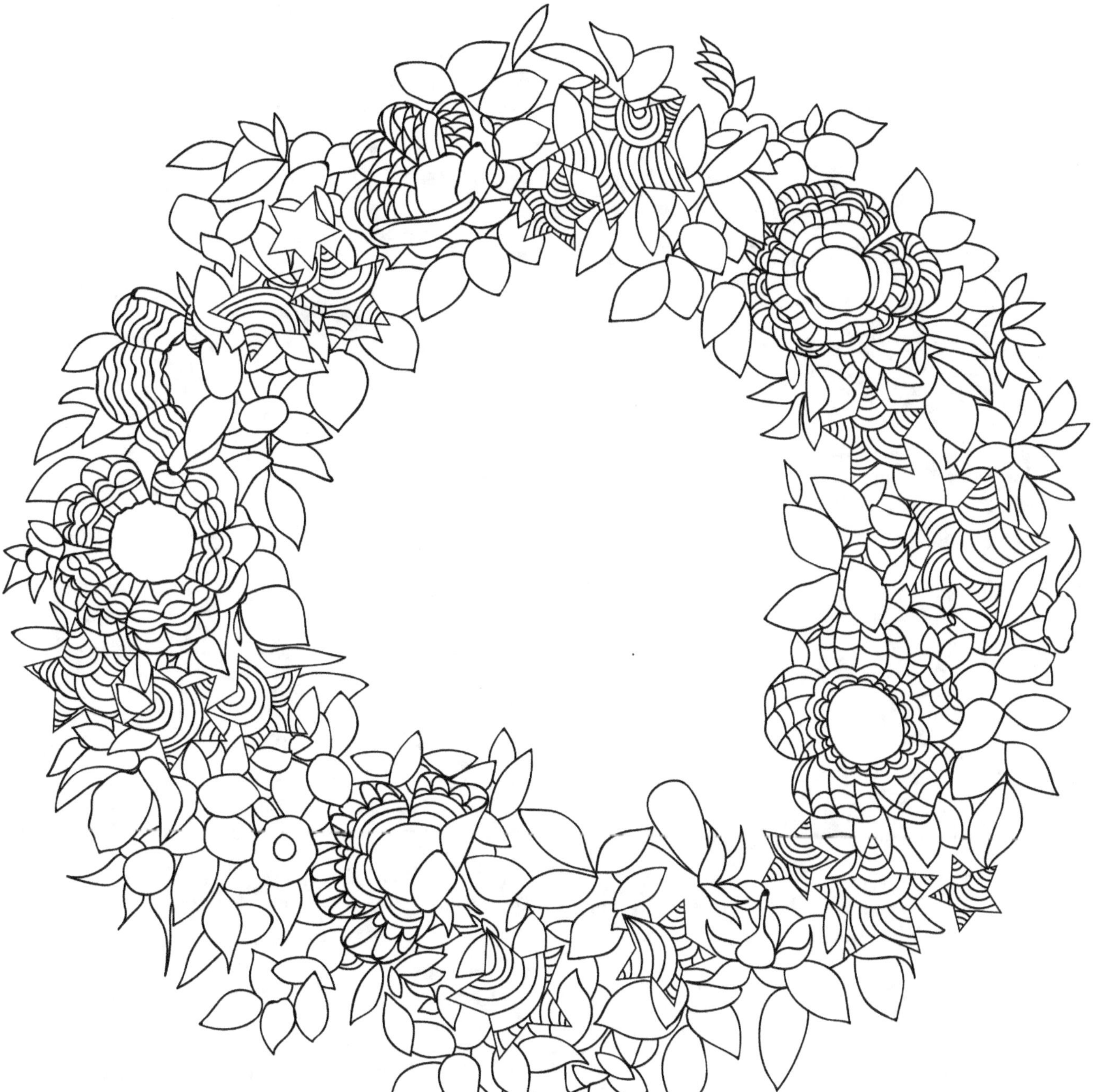

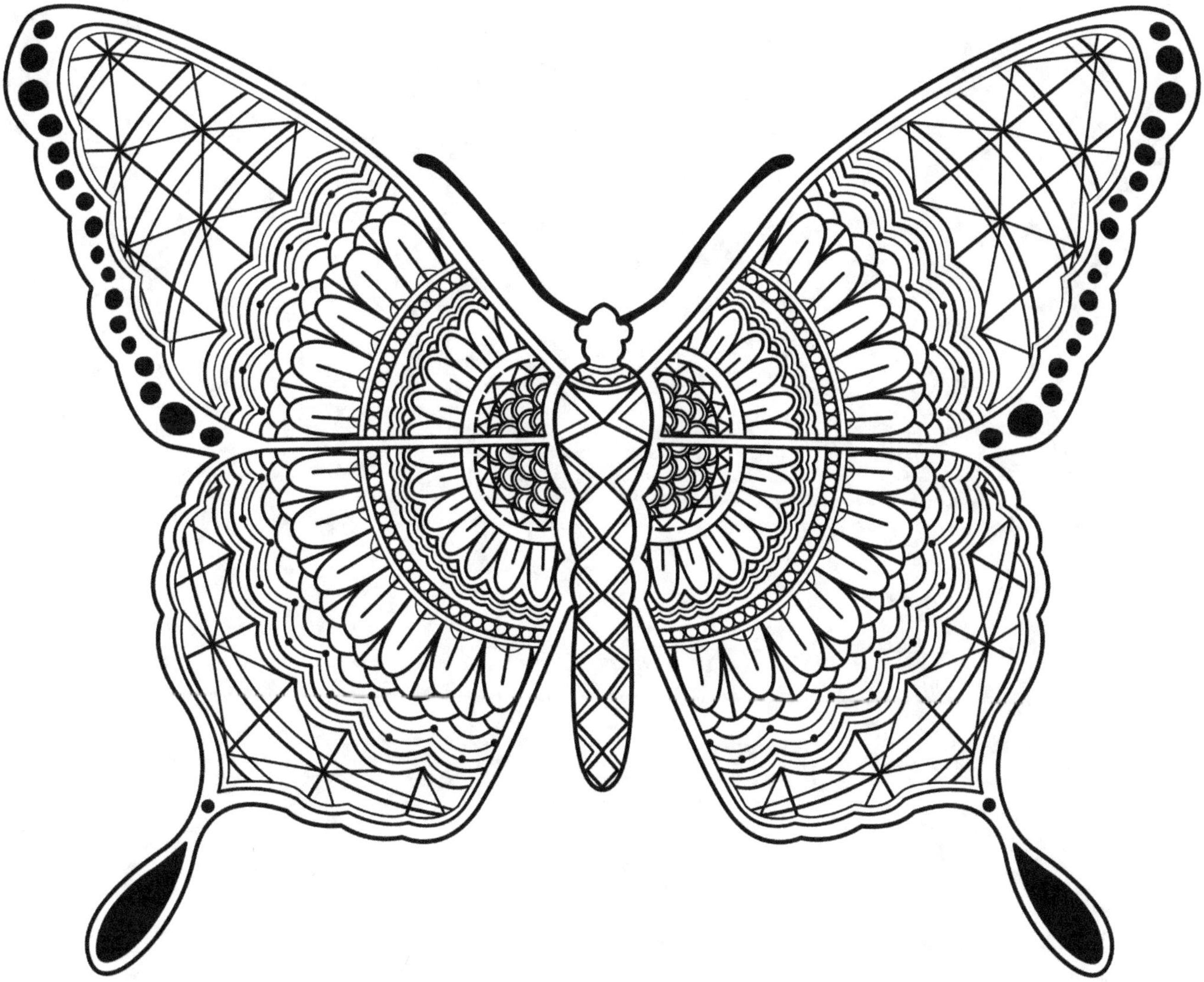

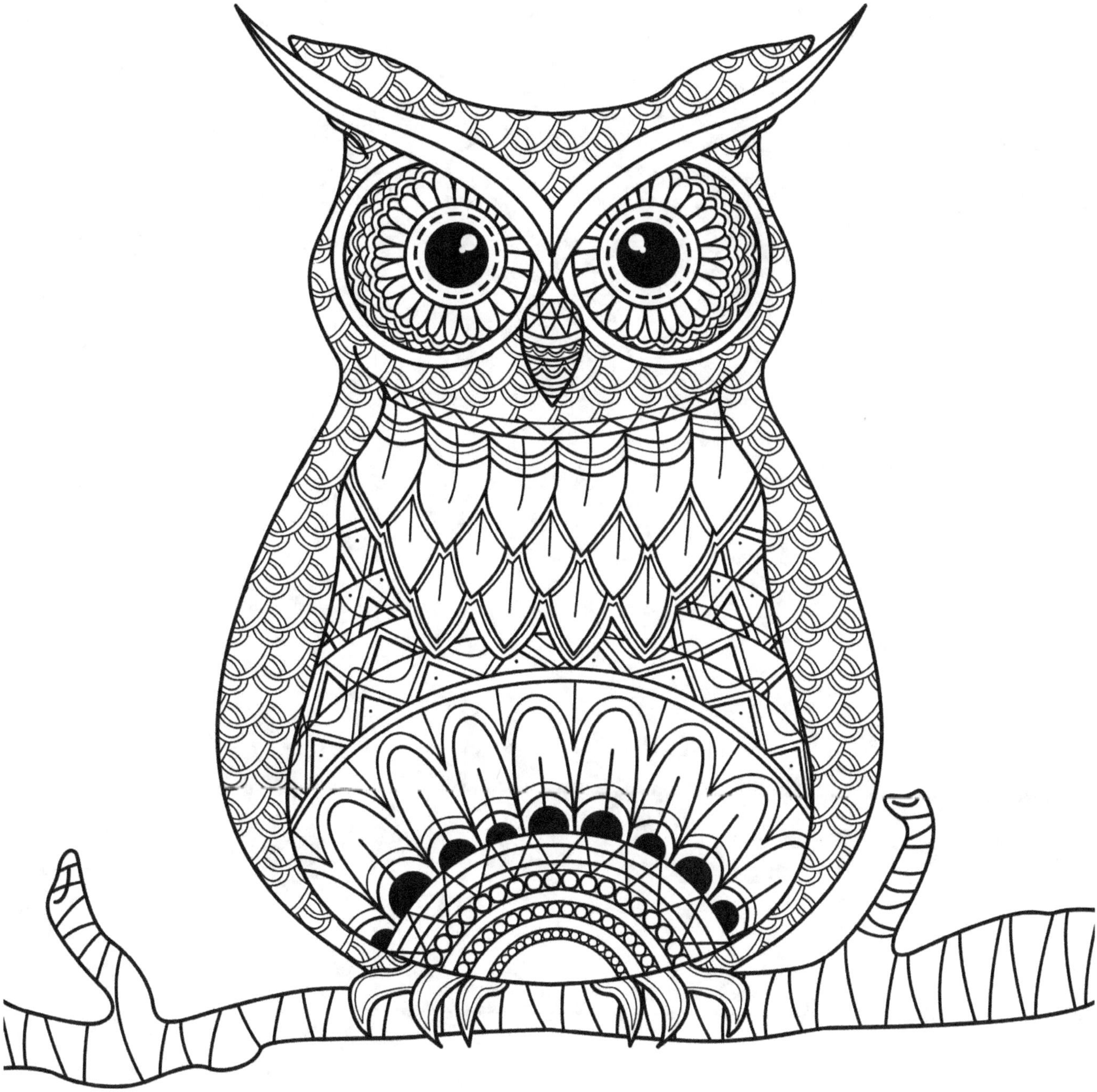

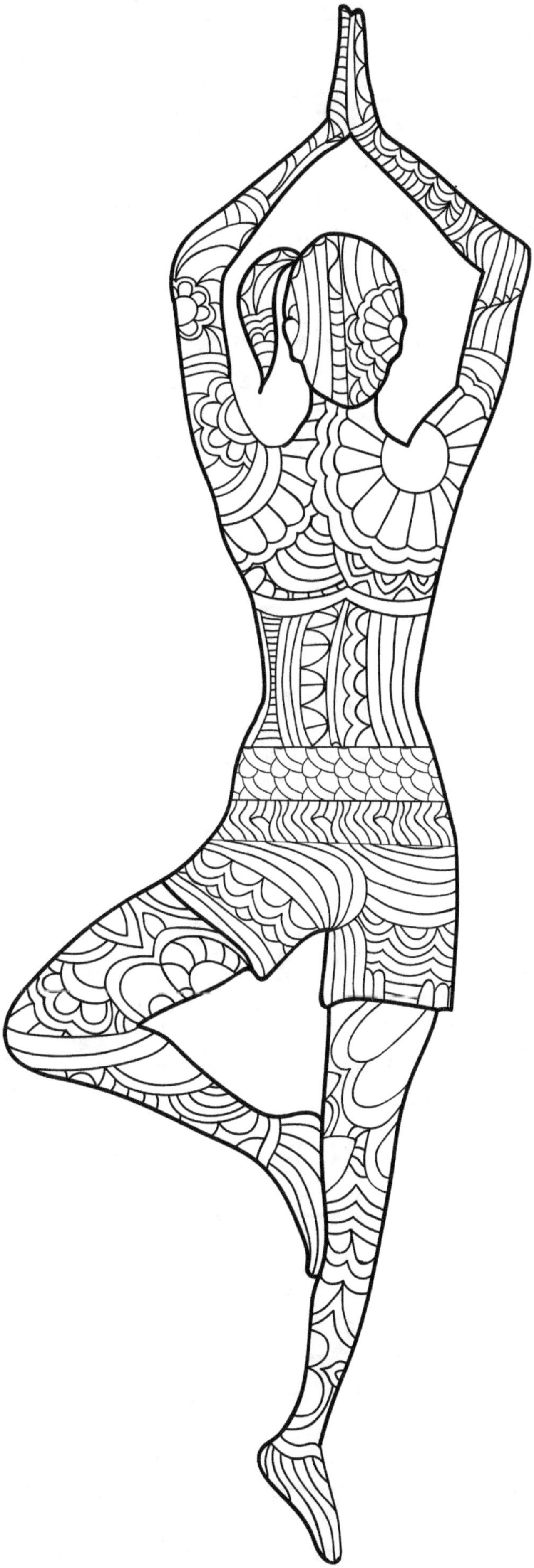

www.ingramcontent.com/pod-product-compliance
Lightning Source LLC
Chambersburg PA
CBHW081132180526
45170CB00008B/3074
9781523353231